NOTES TO USERS
NOTES TO USERS

THESE Notes are complementary to
A.P. 2095 Pilot's Notes General and assume
a thorough knowledge of its contents. All
pilots should be in possession of a copy of
A.P. 2095 (see A.M.O. A.718/48).

Additional copies may be obtained by the
Station Publications Officer by application on
R.A.F. Form 294A, in duplicate, to Com-
mand headquarters for onward transmission
to A.P.F.S. (see A.P. 113). The number of
this publication must be quoted in full—
A.P. 1691D—P.N.

Comments and suggestions should be for-
warded through the usual channels to the
Air Ministry (T.F.2).

HARVARD 2B

AIR MINISTRY
March, 1949
(Reprinted—April, 1951)

Air Publication 1691D—P.N.
2nd Edition
Pilot's Notes

HARVARD 2B

LIST OF CONTENTS

PART I—DESCRIPTIVE　　*Para.*

PART IV—EMERGENCIES

PART V—ILLUSTRATIONS

HAVARD 2B

PILOT'S CHECK LIST

(Excluding checks of Operational Equipment)

ITEM	CHECK
1. Weight and balance.	Within permissible limits.
2. Authorisation book.	Sign.
3. Form 700.	Sign.

External checks.

N.B.—Start at the port wing root trailing edge and work clockwise around the aircraft.

ITEM	CHECK
4. Port mainplane.	Condition of upper surface. Fuel filler cap secure. Condition of stub wing fairing.
5. Port flap.	Condition and position.
6. Port aileron.	Condition. Condition of trimmer. External control lock removed.
7. Port navigation lights.	Condition.
8. Port mainplane.	Condition of under surface. Lashing ring removed. External aerial secure. Panels secure. Condition of leading edge. Condition of landing lights.
9. Port undercarriage.	Extension of oleo leg. Condition of undercarriage wheel bay. Wheel disc secure. Brake lead secure. Tyre for cuts and creep. Chock in position.
10. Engine.	Condition of propeller and counterweights. Cowlings and panels secure. Absence of oil leaks. Condition and security of exhaust pipe.
11. External fire-extinguisher(s).	In position.
12. Centreplane.	Condition of under surface. External aerial secure.
13. Starboard undercarriage.	Extension of oleo leg. Condition of undercarriage wheel bay. Wheel disc secure. Brake lead secure. Tyre for cuts and creep. Chock in position.

ITEM	CHECK		ITEM	CHECK
14. Starboard main-plane.	Condition of under surface. Lashing ring removed. Panels secure. Condition of leading edge. Condition of landing light.		23. Rudder.	Condition. Condition of trimmer. External control lock removed.
			24. Tailwheel.	Extension of oleo leg. Tyre for cuts and creep.
15. Starboard navigation lights.	Condition.		25. Port elevator.	Condition. Condition of trimmer. External control lock removed.
16. Starboard aileron.	Condition. Condition of trimmer. External control lock removed.		26. Port tailplane.	Condition of upper and lower surfaces. Condition of leading edge.
17. Starboard flap.	Condition and position.			
18. Starboard main-plane.	Condition of upper surface. Fuel filler cap secure. Condition of stub wing fairing.		27. Port fuselage.	Condition. Panels secure. External aerial secure.
19. Starboard fuselage.	Condition. Panels secure. External aerials secure. Condition of under surface. Condition of identification lights.		28. Baggage compartment.	Security of equipment. First-aid outfit stowed. Starting handle and lashing rings stowed. Door shut.
			29. Dispersal area.	All clear around aircraft.
20. Starboard tailplane.	Condition of upper and lower surfaces. Condition of leading edge.		N.B.—If the aircraft is to be flown solo carry out the following checks in the rear cockpit.	
			30. Rear compartment.	No loose equipment.
21. Starboard elevator.	Condition. Condition of trimmer. External control lock removed.		31. Safety harness.	Secured.
22. Fin.	Condition. Condition of leading edge. Condition of tail lights.		32. Fire-extinguisher.	In position.
			33. Control column.	Stowed.

	ITEM	CHECK		ITEM	CHECK
34.	Rear sliding hood.	Jettison levers flush with panels and locking wires in position. Locked shut.	48.	Undercarriage indicator.	Operation.
			49.	Carburettor heat control.	Movement of selector lever. Set to cold.

Front cockpit checks.

N.B.—Switch on the battery switch and then work from left to right.

	ITEM	CHECK		ITEM	CHECK
			50.	Cockpit lighting switches.	Set as required.
35.	Port fuel gauge.	Switch on lights. Contents.	51.	Navigation lights switch.	Set as required.
36.	Fuel cock.	Reserve tank.	52.	Landing lights switches.	Operation. Switch off.
37.	Undercarriage selector lever.	Down. Green lights on.	53.	Pressure head heater switch.	Off.
38.	Hydraulic handpump.	Pump flaps down and up.	54.	Oil dilution switch.	Off.
39.	Flap selector lever.	Up.	55.	Bomb master switch.	Off.
40.	Fuel handpump.	Check operation with fuel pressure gauge (and warning light, if fitted).	56.	Tail light switch.	Set as required.
			57.	Generator main line switch.	Wired on.
41.	Elevator trimming control.	Full and correct movement. Set to neutral.	58.	Ignition switches.	Off.
42.	Rudder trimming control.	Full and correct movement. Set to neutral.	59.	Oil cooler shutter control.	Movement of selector. Set as required.
43.	R.p.m. control lever.	Max. r.p.m. position.	60.	Direction indicator.	Caged.
44.	Mixture control.	Rich.	61.	Fuel pressure warning light (if fitted).	On.
45.	Throttle.	Closed. Adjust friction.			
46.	Hydraulic pressure gauge.	Zero reading.	62.	Boost gauge.	Static reading.
47.	Flap indicator.	Reading.	63.	Priming pump.	Off.

ITEM	CHECK
64. Gun/ camera air pressure gauge.	Reading.
65. Camera master switch.	Off.
66. Downward identification lights switches.	Set as required.
67. Fire warning light.	Out.
68. Magnetic compass.	Serviceability.
69. Compass lights.	Test.
70. Cockpit heating control.	Set as required.
71. Beam approach control unit.	Switched off.
72. Starboard fuel gauge.	Contents. Switch off lights.
73. Gun/cine camera selector.	Set as required.
74. Flying controls.	Internal control lock off (forward). Gun firing push-button safe. Full and correct movement. Adjust rudder pedals for reach.
75. Pilot's seat.	Adjust for height.
76. Cockpit hood.	Freedom of movement. Jettison levers flush with panels, and locking wires in position.

ITEM	CHECK
Start and warm up the engine (see para. 35).	
77. Fuel cock.	Left-hand tank.
78. Flaps.	Lower. Indicator reading. Hydraulic pressure reading. Raise. Selector up.
79. Direction indicator.	Set with magnetic compass. Uncage.
80. Radio.	Test V.H.F. and other radio aids. Check altimeter setting with control.
81. Fuel pressure warning light (if fitted).	Out.
Exercise and test the engine (see para. 36).	
82. Fuel cock.	Right-hand tank.
83. Chocks.	Clear.
84. Taxying.	As soon as possible test brakes. Direction indicator for accuracy. Artificial horizon for accuracy. Check temperatures and pressures. Pressure head heater on if required.
Checks before take-off.	
85. Trim elevator.	Slightly back (11 o'clock).
Rudder.	Fully right.
86. Mixture.	Fully rich.

	ITEM	CHECK
87.	Carburettor air intake.	As required.
88.	R.p.m. control lever.	Max r.p.m. position. Adjust friction.
89.	Fuel.	Contents. Cock setting.
90.	Flaps.	Up. 15° down for shortest run.
91.	Oil cooler shutter.	As required.
92.	Harness.	Tight and locked.
93.	Engine.	Clear.

Checks in flight as necessary.

Checks before landing—reduce speed to 110 knots.

	ITEM	CHECK
94.	Harness.	Tight and locked.
95.	Fuel.	Contents and cock setting.
96.	Carburettor air intake.	As required.
97.	Mixture.	Fully rich.
98.	Undercarriage.	Down and locked. Green lights on.
99.	Brakes.	Test by depressing the pedals.
100.	R.p.m. control lever.	Set at the 2,000 r.p.m. position.
101.	Flaps.	As required.

After landing. Clear runway.

	ITEM	CHECK
102.	Brakes.	Test.
103.	Flaps.	Up. Selector up.
104.	Pressure head heater.	As required.

On reaching dispersal.

Idle the engine for one minute at 800 r.p.m. or until the cylinder head temperature falls below 205°C., whichever is the longer. (See also para. 50).

	ITEM	CHECK
105.	Mixture control.	Fully forward.

When the engine has stopped.

	ITEM	CHECK
106.	Ignition switches.	Off.
107.	Fuel cock.	Off.
108.	Electrical services.	All off.
109.	Battery switch.	Off.
110.	Direction indicator	Caged.
111.	Internal control lock.	On (lever back).
112.	Chocks.	In position.
113.	Brakes.	Off.
114.	Pressure head cover.	On.
115.	Form 700.	Sign if necessary.
116.	Authorisation book.	Sign.

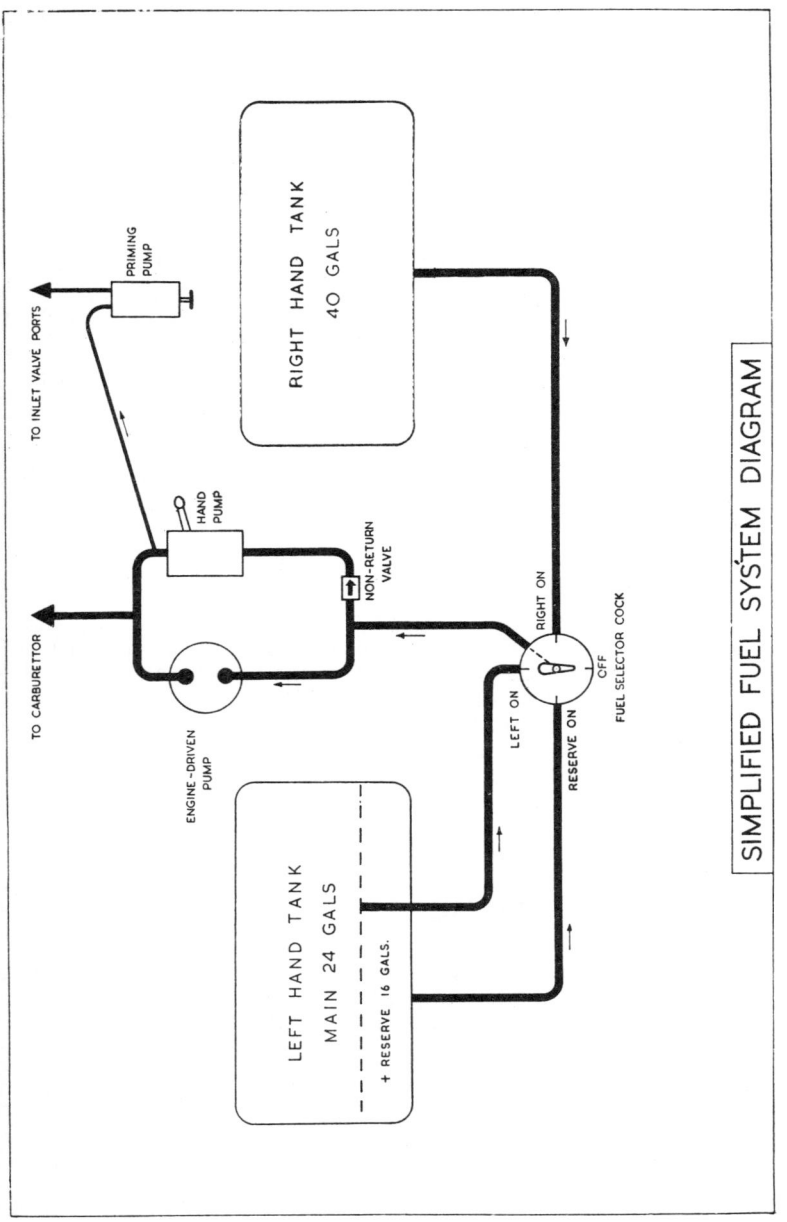

SIMPLIFIED FUEL SYSTEM DIAGRAM

PART I

DESCRIPTIVE

NOTE.—Throughout the publication the following conventions apply:—

(a) Words in capital letters indicate the actual markings on the control concerned.

(b) The numbers quoted in brackets after items in the text refer to the illustrations in Part V, which depict the front cockpit only.

(c) Unless otherwise stated all speeds quoted are indicated airspeeds.

(d) All gallons quoted are Imperial gallons.

INTRODUCTION

1   The Harvard 2B is an advanced trainer fitted with dual controls in tandem and equipped for gunnery and bombing. It is a metal monoplane with fabric-covered control surfaces, and powered by a 550 h.p. Wasp R-1340-AN-1 engine directly driving a two bladed Hamilton counter-weight, constant-speed propeller.

FUEL AND OIL SYSTEMS

2.   Fuel tanks and gauges

The total fuel capacity is 92 gallons in two 46-gallon wing tanks, but these can only be completely filled with the aircraft in a tail-up position. In the normal tail-down position, only 40 gallons can be put into each tank. A stand-pipe in the port tank holds 16 gallons in reserve. Direct reading gauges (58 & 76) are fitted on the front cockpit floor on each side of the pilot's seat. A light switch (at 2) is provided for these gauges in both cockpits, but the gauges can only be accurately read from the front seat.

3. Fuel cocks

A four-position selector cock (36) on the port side of each cockpit is marked OFF, RESERVE ON, LEFT ON, and RIGHT ON. The selector cocks are interconnected.

4. Fuel pumps and pressure gauge

(i) A handpump lever (40) is provided on the port side of each cockpit; the levers being interconnected. The handpump is used when starting the engine and as an alternative to or in support of the engine-driven pump.

(ii) A priming pump (19) is fitted at the top right-hand side of the instrument panel of the front cockpit only. If a Ki-gass pump is fitted the handle is locked by pushing in and screwing to the right. If a Parker pump is fitted, the handle is pushed in and turned to the right to lock, and pushed in before turning to unlock.

(iii) There is a fuel pressure gauge (at 15) at the top right-hand side of the instrument panel, and on some aircraft there may be a separate warning light on the instrument panel which indicates when the pressure falls appreciably below normal (3-5 lb./sq. in.).

5. Oil system

The oil tank holds $8\frac{1}{2}$ gallons of oil with $1\frac{1}{2}$ gallons air space. In the front cockpit only, an oil cooler shutter control (30) is mounted below the instrument panel, and an oil dilution switch is fitted in the bank of switches (2) on the left of the panel.

MAIN SERVICES

6. Hydraulic system

(i) The undercarriage and flaps are operated by the main power-driven hydraulic system, with its alternative handpump. The tailwheel is not retractable. A secondary, master-unit type, hydraulic system is used for brake operation. In the main system a lever (33) on the port side of each cockpit marked POWER CONTROL PUSH cuts in the engine-driven pump; these levers are interconnected. It is more convenient to operate this before

13

moving the flaps or undercarriage selector. The power control returns to the idle position of its own accord after one or two minutes. A pressure gauge (54) on the port side of the front cockpit only shows the output pressure of the engine-driven pump or the handpump. After pushing the power control, the gauge will read 900 to 1,000 lb./sq. in., but should return to zero when the power control returns to the idle position. If it does not, the system is defective, and continuous operation under pressure may then damage the pump.

(ii) The handpump (55) on the port side of the seat in the front cockpit only may be used without pushing the power control; the handle should be pulled out and rotated anti-clockwise to lock it in the extended position.

7. Suction system

An engine-driven pump operates the gyro instruments. There is a suction gauge (6) on the lower left-hand side of the instrument panel.   The normal suction is $3\frac{1}{2}$-$4\frac{1}{2}$ in. of Hg.

8. Pneumatic system

Compressed air, stored in a cylinder behind the rear seat, is used only to operate the camera and the single gun. No engine-driven compressor is fitted, and the available pressure is shown by the gauge (24) on the lower right-hand side of the front instrument panel.

9. Electrical system

(i) A 750-watt generator charges a 12-volt battery which supplies the usual lighting and other services. If either a gyro gun sight or tunable beam approach equipment is fitted, two 12-volt batteries are used in parallel. An external supply socket is fitted on the port side of the fuselage above the wing leading edge.

(ii) An electrical panel on the left-hand side of the instrument panel includes an ammeter (48), a battery switch (51) and a generator main line switch (47) which is normally wired ON. The ammeter shows the generator output and the reading varies according to the services used. It may be as low as 5 amps. if the batteries are fully charged and no services are switched on, or as high as 50 amps. with the services on. If 50 amps. is exceeded and cannot be reduced by switching the services off, the generator main line switch should be turned OFF. The batteries can be isolated when the engine is running, by means of the battery switch. The panel in the rear cockpit carries only rear cockpit lighting and fuel gauge light switches.

(iii) Spare bulbs are stowed on the rear cockpit floor. The fuses are not accessible in flight. If a short-circuit is suspected, turn OFF both battery and generator main line switches.

AIRCRAFT CONTROLS

10. Flying controls

The rear control column is detachable and stows in a socket on the starboard side of the cockpit. The controls are locked by first placing the control column in the fully forward and central position, centralizing the rudder bar, and then pulling up the handle (29) in the front cockpit to the left of the control column. The rudder pedals (31) are adjustable by foot-operated release levers (59) on the inboard side of each pedal. Care must be taken to see that the pedals are in corresponding holes after adjustment.

11. Brakes

Each main wheel brake may be independently operated by pressure on its respective toe pedal in either cockpit. Movement of the rudder pedals alone does not affect the brakes. The brakes are applied for parking by depressing the pedals, pulling out the PARK BRAKE knob (20), on the right-hand side of the instrument panel in the front cockpit only, releasing the pedals, and then releasing the knob. This knob has very little movement. The brakes are disengaged by depressing the pedals in either cockpit. The single cylinder type brakes fitted cannot be relied upon to hold the aircraft when parked facing uphill.

12. Steerable tailwheel

The tailwheel is steerable over the full range of rudder movement, being held in the steerable position by a spring-loaded cam.

To assist manœuvring in a confined space, the cam mechanism will unlock when the angle between the tailwheel and the fore and aft axis of the aircraft exceeds approximately 25°, thus allowing the wheel to caster freely.

Normally sharp application of brake as well as rudder will be required to unlock the cam, but sudden application of opposite rudder when turning may also cause unlocking.

13. Trimming tab controls

The elevator handwheel (38) on the port side operates in the natural sense. The rudder handwheel (39) is on the same axis and is turned forward to apply right trim. There is a notch in each handwheel, and the neutral positions are with both notches vertical. The controls are fitted in each cockpit.

14. Undercarriage control

(i) The undercarriage lever (56) on the port side of each cockpit has two normal positions only, UP and DOWN. In the DOWN position a stud on the lever (in the front cockpit only) engages in a notch on the quadrant. This lever must be lifted to disengage the stud and then moved smartly back to raise the undercarriage. If the lever is moved slowly it may stick due to the hydraulic pressure reaching the jacks before the locks are disengaged. If this occurs the lever should be returned to the DOWN position for a few seconds and then moved quickly back again.

(ii) The fully-forward position of the undercarriage lever marked EMERGENCY PUSH HANDLE DOWN TO ENGAGE PIN is for use only if the wheels are down, but the lights indicate that the locks are not engaged. The lever then engages the locking pins manually. Care must be taken to ensure that it is not inadvertently moved into this position when lowering the undercarriage normally. If this is done it should be returned immediately to the normal DOWN position, or the locking pins may be damaged by the legs when lowering is nearly completed. The undercarriage can be raised, and the emergency fully-forward position operated only from the front cockpit. The undercarriage may be lowered from either cockpit.

15. **Undercarriage position indicator and warning light**

A standard electrical indicator (46) is fitted in the front cockpit to the left of the electrical panel and in the rear cockpit at the top of the instrument panel. Indications are:—

Two green lights	...	Both wheels locked down.
Two red lights	...	Both wheels unlocked.
No lights ...	...	Both wheels locked up.

In addition, both cockpits have on the top left-hand side of the instrument panel a red warning light (11) which comes on whenever the undercarriage is not locked down, and the throttle is less than one-third open.

16. **Flap control and indicator**

The flap lever (57) adjacent to the undercarriage lever in each cockpit has three positions UP, LOCK, and DOWN. These levers are interconnected. To obtain an intermediate position of the flaps, the lever should be moved UP or DOWN as required, and then moved to the LOCK position when the flaps have reached their desired setting. A mechanical indicator (53) reading in "degrees" is fitted on the port side of each cockpit. Unlike the undercarriage lever, the flap lever is designed to be moved to the UP position without first being lifted.

ENGINE CONTROLS

17. **Throttle**

The throttle lever (4) moves in a quadrant on the port side of each cockpit wall. The quadrant is gated at the take-off position and has a friction nut (45) at the side. There is no automatic boost control.

18. Mixture control

The mixture control (41) adjacent to the throttle is manually operated and is served by the same friction nut (45). It is moved over a range from RICH (fully back) through increasing weak mixture to the cut-out position (fully forward). In the front cockpit only, a catch on the throttle draws the mixture lever back to the RICH position as the throttle is closed. This catch can be released and the mixture control lever moved fully forward to stop the engine.

19. Propeller control

The r.p.m. control lever (43) is adjacent to the mixture control and again is served by the throttle friction nut (45). The fully aft position gives POSITIVE COARSE PITCH; in all other positions of the lever the propeller is under constant speed control, the range being from about 1,400 to 2,250 r.p.m. POSITIVE COARSE PITCH will give lower r.p.m. than 1,400 at low airspeeds.

20. Air intake heat control

This control (1) is below the electrical panel in the front cockpit only and may be set to any desired position (see para. 40 (iv)).

21. Engine instruments

Boost gauge (17), r.p.m. indicator (18), and a combined oil pressure, oil temperature, and fuel pressure gauge (15) and a cylinder head temperature gauge (10) are all mounted on both instrument panels. A carburettor mixture thermometer (9) is fitted on the front instrument panel only. In the rear cockpit it is replaced by a clock.

22. Ignition switch.

This switch (7) on the left-hand side of each instrument panel has four positions: OFF, L, R, BOTH. The two switches are mechanically interconnected.

23. Starting equipment

(i) An inertia starter is fitted. A 3-position switch (27) at the bottom of the instrument panel (front cockpit only) is

(iii) Each cockpit has a red emergency light (top left of each instrument panel) operated from a pair of dry cells stowed in a canvas pocket (34) to the left of the front seat. Each light has a separate switch (49) on the left of the instrument panel.

28. External lights

(i) The navigation lights are operated by a switch on the left of the row (at 2) in the front cockpit only. When this switch is ON, a separate tail light switch (52) operates the tail lights.

(ii) The next two switches in this row separately control the landing lamps mounted in the port and starboard leading edges.

(iii) A switch box (67) on the right of the front cockpit controls the white signalling lamp, and the red, green and amber identification lamps mounted beneath the rear fuselage. The switches are placed in the down position to give a steady light; in the up position, morse can be transmitted when the key on top of the box is operated.

29. Radio controls

(i) A 4-channel V.H.F. transmitter-receiver incorporating intercom. is used, with its press-button type control unit (32) fitted on the port side of the front cockpit. On R.A.F. 2B's a press-to-transmit switch (62) is fitted inside the spade grip of the front control column. In the rear cockpit, it is at the top of the control column, and a press-to-mute switch is fitted below. On Naval 2B's, however, these switches are repositioned as follows:
In the front cockpit the press-to-transmit and the bomb-firing controls are reversed. The transmit button being on the throttle at (42), and the bomb-firing switch being on the stick at (62) and in the rear cockpit the transmit button is above the throttle on the port coaming. Two press-to-mute switches are fitted, one in each cockpit above the throttle.

(ii) The control unit (71) for the tunable beam approach equipment is fitted on the starboard side of the front cockpit, with its tuning control (69) mounted above.

30. Armament equipment

(i) The single gun in the starboard wing is operated by compressed air, controlled by the selector valve (74), on the starboard side and slightly aft of the front cockpit seat. The selector has four positions marked OFF, GUN & CAMERA CINE, GUN, and CAMERA CINE. Provided that the gun firing pushbutton (63) on the front control column only is set to FIRE, the gun will fire with

FINAL CHECKS FOR TAKE-OFF

TRIM   ... ELEVATOR : SLIGHTLY BACK (11 O'CLOCK)

RUDDER : FULLY RIGHT

MIXTURE   ... FULL RICH

PROP.   ... MAX. R.P.M.

FUEL   ... CHECK CONTENTS

CORRECT TANK SELECTED

FLAPS   ... UP OR 15° DOWN

FINAL CHECKS FOR LANDING

FUEL ... CHECK CONTENTS
CORRECT TANK
SELECTED

MIXTURE ... FULL RICH

WHEELS ... DOWN AND LOCKED
GREEN LIGHTS ON

BRAKES ... PARK BRAKE OFF
TEST

PROP. ... 2,000 R.P.M.

FLAPS ... AS REQUIRED

the selector set to either GUN or GUN & CAMERA CINE.

(ii) A G.45 cine camera is fitted in the port wing, and may be operated in two ways:—(a) by pressing the gun firing pushbutton, provided that the camera master switch (65) is ON, and the selector is set to either GUN & CAMERA CINE, or CAMERA CINE, or (b) by pressing the camera pushbutton (64) with the G.45 camera master switch ON, and irrespective of the setting of the selector. The camera footage indicator (61) is fitted below the camera master switch.

(iii) A gyro gun sight (14) is fitted in the front cockpit, with its range control (4) on the throttle lever, and a SELECTOR DIMMER switch (35) at the rear of the left-hand control shelf. The G.G.S. master switch (25) is on the right-hand side of the instrument panel.

(iv) A G.G.S. camera recorder can be fitted above the gun sight and is operated by the pushbutton (64) on the front control column, provided that the G.G.S. master switch is on.

(v) In the rear cockpit a ring and bead sight is fitted.

(vi) The bomb release button (42) is mounted in the end of the throttle lever in the front cockpit, and the bomb selector switches (22), and the bomb jettison switch (66) on the right of the instrument panel. The BOMB MASTER SWITCH (50) must be ON before the bombs can be either released normally or jettisoned.

31. **Static pressure selector switch.**

If this switch (23) is still fitted, it should be locked in the "pressure head" position.

32. **Two-stage screening**

The "fixed" screens are fitted on the ground to the top and sides of the front cockpit, and a folding front screen (which may be fitted in the air) is carried in a stowage (73) to the right of the front seat. The map case (72) is re-positioned behind this stowage. To eliminate misting-up of the two-stage goggles, the extractor tube of the goggles in use is plugged into one of the two vent holes (37) in the fuselage wall on the port side of the front seat. Stowage (75) for these goggles is provided on the starboard side of the front cockpit.

PART II

HANDLING

34. Management of the fuel system

(i) Tanks may be selected in any convenient order, but if all are full, the recommended order is RIGHT, LEFT, RESERVE. When flying at low altitude, change from RIGHT to LEFT when the right gauge shows 10 gallons, and from LEFT to RESERVE when the left gauge shows 25 gallons.

At a safe height the LEFT or RIGHT tanks may remain selected until the fuel pressure drops. If the engine cuts, the throttle should be closed before another cock setting is selected to avoid overspeeding of the propeller, and the handpump should be used to assist the engine to pick up.

(ii) The handpump may be used in flight as described above, for priming the fuel system before starting, and at any time should the fuel pressure drop appreciably below normal.

35. Starting and warming up the engine

(i) After carrying out the external, internal and cockpit checks detailed in the Pilot's Check List, confirm:

Fuel cock	Reserve tank.
Throttle	$\frac{1}{2}$ inch open.
Mixture control	Rich (fully back).
R.p.m. control lever ...	Max. r.p.m. position.
Carburettor heat control ...	COLD.
Oil cooler shutter	As required.
Ignition switch	OFF.
Battery switch	ON.

(ii) Have the propeller turned through two revolutions by hand to check for hydraulic locking.

(iii) If the engine is to be started from an external source, have a ground starter battery plugged in and switched on.

(iv) Work the handpump to fill the fuel lines and carburettor.

(v) Prime the engine; if it is cold and a Parker type pump is fitted, 4 to 6 strokes are required. If a Ki-gass pump is fitted, 3 to 4 strokes are required. A hot engine should not require priming, or at the most 1 to 2 strokes with the Parker pump or 1 stroke with the Ki-gass pump.

(vi) Switch on the ignition (BOTH) and energise the starter electrically for 12 to 15 seconds or until the hum becomes constant. Never exceed 20 seconds. If the starter is hand-cranked the brushes should first be lifted (see para. 23 (ii)).

(vii) Return the starter switch to the central position, pause for a second and then engage the starter. Keep the starter engaging switch on until the engine is running evenly, as it also operates the booster coil. Ensure that the starter switch is returned to the OFF position immediately the engine is running.

(viii) It may be necessary to continue priming gently, and to operate the handpump to maintain the pressure in the carburettor until the engine picks up.

(ix) If the engine fails to start:—

(a) Wait until the propeller stops rotating, keeping the engaging switch on to ensure that the flywheel stops. Immediately the propeller stops rotating, ensure that the starter switch is returned to the OFF position.

(b) Switch off the ignition.

(c) If the engine has been over-primed, open the throttle fully, move the mixture control forward to the cut-off position and have the propeller turned through several revolutions by hand. It should in any case be turned half a revolution to ensure that the flywheel is not engaging with the engine.

(d) Damage may be caused if the starter switch is set to ENERGISE either with the flywheel running or with it meshed to the engine.

(x) When the engine is firing evenly screw down or lock the priming pump, open the throttle slowly and warm up at 1,000 r.p.m.

(xi) While warming up at 1,000 r.p.m. carry out the checks detailed in the Pilot's Check List, items 77 to 81.

36 Exercising and testing

After warming up to 40°C. oil and 120°C. cylinder head temperatures, adjust the oil cooler shutter as necessary and:—

(i) Test each magneto as a precautionary check before increasing power further.

(ii) Open up to $-2\frac{1}{2}$ lb./sq. in. boost, and check the operation of the constant-speed unit by moving the r.p.m. control lever over the full governing range at least twice. Return the lever fully forward and check the operation of the vacuum pump and that the generator is charging.

(iii) Open up to the static boost reading and check that the r.p.m. are within 50 of the reference figure quoted in the Form 700.

(iv) At the same boost test each magneto by switching from BOTH to R, back to BOTH, BOTH to L, and again back to BOTH. The single ignition drop should not exceed 100 r.p.m. If it does exceed this figure but there is no undue vibration, the ignition should be checked at higher power—see below. If there is marked vibration the engine should be shut down and the cause investigated.

NOTE.—The following full-power checks (v) and (vi) should be carried out after repair, inspection other than daily, or at the discretion of the pilot. Except in these circumstances, no useful purpose will be served by a full-power check.

(v) Open up to the gate and check the boost ($+3$ lb./sq. in.) and r.p.m. (about 2,200 max. 2,250). This check should be as brief as possible.

(vi) Throttle back until the r.p.m. fall, thus ensuring that the propeller is not constant-speeding, and test each magneto. If the single ignition drop exceeds 100 r.p.m. the aircraft should not be flown.

(vii) After completing the checks either at $-2\frac{1}{2}$ lb./sq. in. or at full power, steadily move the throttle to the fully closed position, and check the minimum idling r.p.m., then open up to 1,000 r.p.m.

37. Taxying

(i) Before taxying, carry out the checks detailed in the Pilot's Check List, items 82 to 84.

(ii) The brakes may be fierce, and harsh use while **taxying** may cause the steerable tailwheel to unlock.

38. **Take-off**

(i) Carry out the checks in the Pilot's Check List, items 85 to 93.

(ii) Align the aircraft with the runway, ensuring that the tailwheel is straight.

(iii) Open the throttle smoothly to the gate; there is a slight tendency to swing to port.

(iv) The aircraft should be flown off at approximately 70 knots.

(v) If the flaps are used, raise them at a safe height and before a speed of 110 knots is reached.

39. **Climbing**

(i) The speed for maximum rate of climb is 100 knots to 5,000 feet. Above this height, reduce speed by 5 knots per 5,000 feet, and move the mixture control forward to prevent rough running due to overrichness. As height is gained, open the throttle progressively to maintain $+1\frac{1}{2}$ lb./sq. in. boost at 2,200 r.p.m.

(ii) For maximum range on the climb, fly at 110 knots, using -2 lb./sq. in. boost and 1,850 r.p.m., with the mixture control up to the throttle.

(iii) If cylinder head temperature is excessive, increase speed and keep the mixture control in the fully rich position.

40. **General flying**

(i) Changes of trim:—

Wheels down ...	...	Slightly nose down
Wheels up ...	...	Slightly nose up
Flaps down ...	...	Nose down
Flaps up ...	...	Nose up

(ii) Flying at reduced airspeeds:—
Reduce airspeed to 110 knots, lower 15° of flap and select 2,000 r.p.m. Speed may then be reduced to not less than 75 knots. The stalling speed under these conditions is 55 knots.

(iii) Mixture control.—In general this should be operated as follows:—

    (a) For flying at power in excess of that permitted for weak mixture (-2 lb./sq. in. and 1,850 r.p.m.) the control should only be advanced from the fully rich position as necessary to avoid rough running and loss of power due to overrichness.

    (b) For flying at power below that permitted for weak mixture, the control should be advanced up to but not beyond the throttle. Care must be taken, however, not to render the mixture overweak, which will be shown by a drop in r.p.m. and/or a rise in cylinder head temperature.

    (c) For cruising at moderate and high altitudes, it will be found that beyond a certain throttle opening no further increase in boost or power is obtained. To simplify operation of the mixture control, the throttle should not be advanced beyond this point. Economical mixture strength will still be obtained under these conditions by operating the mixture control as above.

(iv) Use of hot air:—

    (a) Both on the ground and in the air, hot air should be used when airframe icing conditions exist or when the humidity is such that, when combined with the temperature drop through the induction system, it is liable to cause carburettor icing. The hot air intake should then be adjusted to give a reading of $0°C.$ to $+10°C.$ on the carburettor temperature gauge.

    (b) Normally, take-off should be made with the intake control fully cold, but under icing conditions, it is advisable to set the control before take-off to give $+5°C.$ carburettor temperature at about -2 lb./sq. in. boost, and to set it in the same way for the approach.

    (c) A change from cold to hot, or vice versa, should not be made at full power.

41. **Flying for range and endurance**

(i) Flying for maximum range

For maximum range both on the climb and in level flight the recommended speed is 110 knots at − 2 lb./sq. in. boost. The r.p.m. should be 1,850 on the climb, and adjusted to give 110 knots in level flight. As the r.p.m. are varied, it will be necessary to readjust the boost setting. The r.p.m. may be as low as 1,400, but below this figure the generator output may be inadequate. If at low altitude the recommended speed is exceeded at minimum r.p.m., the boost should be reduced accordingly. The use of hot air involves very little loss of range if the mixture control is kept up to the throttle.

(ii) Flying for endurance.

Fly at the lowest practicable altitude. Use the minimum r.p.m. required to keep the generator charging, weak mixture, and the smallest throttle opening at which height can be maintained at 90 knots.

42. **Fuel consumptions**

(i) Consumptions at high power:—

Mixture Control	R.p.m.	Boost lb./sq. in.	Galls./hour
RICH	2,250	+ 3	56
RICH	2,200	+ 1½	48
RICH	1,925	0	30

(ii) Consumption under weak mixture conditions (gallons/hour):—

R.p.m.	Boost lb./sq. in.				
	−2	−3	−4	−5	−6
1,800	26	23½	22	20	17½
1,700	24	22	20½	19	17
1,600	22	21	19	17	16
1,500	20	19	17	16	14
1,400	18	17	15	14	13

(iii) A range curve at 2,000 ft. follows:—

HARVARD 2B

CRUISING A.N.M.P.G. AT 2,000 FEET

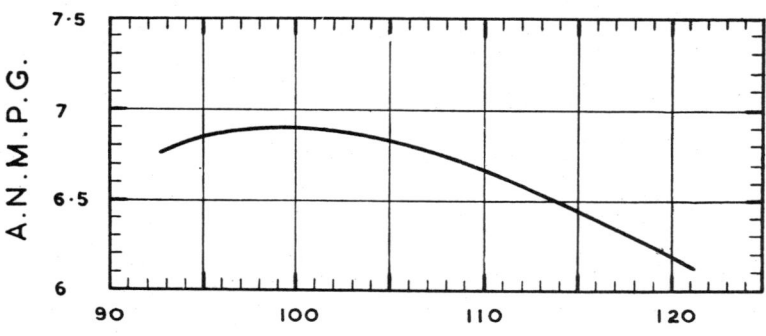

I.A.S. in Knots.

43. Position error correction

From	85	105	120	140	knots
To	105	120	140	160	
Add	2	3	4	5	knots

44. Stalling
(i) The approximate stalling speeds in knots are:—
Power off
        Undercarriage and flaps up   60
        Undercarriage and flaps down 55
Power on
        Under typical landing conditions   50
(ii) There is slight elevator buffeting just before the stall, but this cannot be relied upon to give adequate warning. At the stall, with flaps up or down, the nose and either wing may drop. With flaps down the wing drops more quickly than with flaps up. In both cases, if the stick is held hard back, the aircraft will spin.

(iii) If the aircraft is stalled in a steep turn, buffeting will occur and the aircraft will flick. Recovery is normal and immediate if pressure on the control column is relaxed. The aircraft will spin if the control column is held hard back.

45. Spinning

(i) Both hoods should be closed to avoid panels blowing out of the canopy.

(ii) In either direction the aircraft readily enters the spin. Considerable shuddering occurs for approximately two turns and the spin then becomes smoother. Normal recovery action is effective; the aircraft takes $1\frac{1}{2}$-2 turns to recover, during which time the rate of rotation increases and then stops abruptly. The rudder should then be centralised and the speed allowed to build up to 120 knots before easing out of the dive. In order to avoid overspeeding of the propeller, the throttle should be opened slowly during the recovery.

(iii) Owing to the strain on the undercarriage and flaps, spinning should not be carried out with them down. Should an unintentional spin occur, normal recovery action is effective and should be applied immediately.

46. Diving

(i) Leave the r.p.m. control lever at moderate cruising r.p.m. position and keep the throttle open to give -7 to -5 lb./sq. in. boost. With the throttle so set, 2,250 r.p.m. may be exceeded for 20 seconds with a maximum of 2,650. The boost will rise as height is lost.

(ii) For a dive with the throttle closed, the r.p.m. control lever must be set to the minimum r.p.m. position before closing the throttle and 2,250 r.p.m. must not be exceeded.

47. Aerobatics

(i) The following speeds in knots are recommended:—

Roll	...	...	...	...	130—140
Loop	...	...	...	...	170—180
Half roll off the loop		...	...	190—200

(ii) 1,850 r.p.m. and -2 lb./sq. in. boost is sufficient for all these manœuvres, and the mixture control can be kept up to the throttle.

(iii) If the engine cuts in inverted flight or through negative "g", the throttle should be closed to prevent subsequent overspeeding.

(iv) Overspeeding

During prolonged flight in cold temperatures the oil in the propeller cylinder may congeal sufficiently to make pitch changing sluggish. In these circumstances overspeeding may occur in a dive, due to the reluctance of the propeller to change quickly into a coarser pitch. This may be prevented by moving the r.p.m. control lever over its full range slowly before commencing aerobatic manœuvres.

48. **Approach and landing**

(i) Carry out the checks in the Pilot's Check List, items 94 to 101.

(ii) The recommended speeds in knots at which the airfield boundary should be crossed are:—

				Flaps down	Flaps up
Engine assisted	...	...	...	70—75	75—80
Glide	...	...	...	75—80	80—85

(iii) In a strong cross-wind or in rough weather it is preferable to make a wheel landing. In the three point attitude, particularly with full flap, there is a tendency in these conditions to balloon either before or after touchdown, and control may then be found insufficient.

(iv) After touchdown when the tail is on the ground, the control column should be held hard back; this helps to keep the tailwheel in the steerable position. The application of rudder alone may not always be sufficient to maintain directional control and brake should then be used as necessary. In the event of a swing occurring, rudder should only be used consistent with the effective use of brake.

49. **Mislanding and going round again**

(i) Open up to 0 lb./sq. in. boost. If more power is required, move the r.p.m. control lever fully forward before opening up to +3 lb./sq. in.

(ii) Raise the undercarriage and retrim.

(iii) Climb initially at 80-85 knots. At a safe height raise the flaps in stages and retrim. The flaps will start to come up when the flap lever is moved, even if the power control has not been pressed.

50. **After landing**

(i) Before taxying, carry out the checks detailed in the Pilot's Check List, items 102 to 104.

(ii) After reaching dispersal, idle the engine at about 800 r.p.m. for about a minute, or until the cylinder head temperature falls below 205°C., whichever is the longer.

Then test each magneto and move the mixture control fully forward past the throttle catch.

NOTE.—(a) If the serviceability of the engine is in doubt, it should be checked by carrying out such items of the run-up given in para. 36 as may be necessary. Before the engine is stopped, it should then be idled at 800 r.p.m. for at least one minute, or until the cylinder head temperature falls below 205°C. whichever is the longer, and, if the ignition has not already been checked, the magnetos should be tested for a dead cut before stopping the engine.

(b) The oil dilution period for this aircraft is 1 to 3 minutes.

(c) In very cold weather, the r.p.m. control lever should be set to the minimum r.p.m. position, and the throttle opened sufficiently to allow the pitch to change to fully coarse; otherwise, oil would solidify around the exposed portions of the propeller barrel.

(iii) When the engine has stopped, carry out the checks detailed in the Pilot's Check List, items 106 to 116.

PART III
LIMITATIONS

51. **Engine data**

	R.p.m.	Boost lb./sq. in.	Temp. °C. Cyl.	Oil	Mixture control
MAX. TAKE-OFF (5 MIN. LIMIT)	2,250	+3	260	85	RICH
MAX. CLIMB (CONTINUOUS)	2,200	+1½	260	85	RICH*
MAX. CRUISING (CONTINUOUS)	1,925	−½	230	85	RICH*
MAX. WEAK (CONTINUOUS)	1,850	−2	230	85	Up to the throttle.

DESIRED
TEMPERATURES   205   50/70
DIVING:—

The maximum r.p.m. are 2,650; 2,250 r.p.m. to be exceeded only for 20 seconds and then with the throttle not less than one-third open.
*At altitude, it may be necessary to advance the mixture control to avoid overrichness.

OIL PRESSURE:—
MAXIMUM   ...   .   100 lb./sq. in.
NORMAL   ...   .   70 to 90 lb./sq. in.
MINIMUM CRUISING   ...   50 lb./sq. in.
MINIMUM IDLING ...   ...   10 lb./sq. in.

TEMPERATURES:—
MINIMUM FOR TAKE-OFF   ...   ...   OIL +40°C.
                                                        CYL. 120°C.
MAXIMUM BEFORE TAKE-OFF   ...   CYL. 205°C.
MAXIMUM FOR STOPPING ENGINE   CYL. 205°C.
FUEL PRESSURE
NORMAL   ...   .   3-5 lb./sq. in.

52. **Flying limitations**

(i) Maximum speeds in knots:—

Diving   225
Undercarriage lowering   130
Undercarriage locked down   145
Flaps down   110

(ii) Full use of ailerons may be made up to 165 knots; thereafter they should be used with care, particularly when "g" is applied.

(iii) Certain conditions of loading may bring the C.G. behind the aft limit and before flight it should be checked that the loading is in accordance with the current loading diagram.

PART IV
EMERGENCIES

53. **Undercarriage emergency operation**

(i) If the undercarriage fails to go down by normal power operation, leave the undercarriage selector **DOWN** and operate the handpump until solid resistance is felt, and the green lights come on.

(ii) If both power and handpump fail, the undercarriage will come down under its own weight with the lever in the DOWN position. It will, however, be necessary to yaw the aircraft slightly from side to side to throw the undercarriage legs into their locked positions.

(iii) If doubt exists as to whether the undercarriage legs are down, it should be possible to establish the position of the down lock(s) by looking through the perspex panels fitted in the upper surfaces of each mainplane. Every effort must be made by yawing the aircraft and similar manœuvres to ensure that the undercarriage legs are down before the lever is moved to the emergency position (see para. 14 (ii)).

(iv) If the undercarriage is down, but the green lights do not come on, indicating that the spring-loaded down locks are not engaged, lift and move the undercarriage lever fully forward to the **EMERGENCY** position, when the locks will be engaged manually. The green lights can only show when the undercarriage is fully down and the down locks are right home.

54. **Flap emergency operation**

If the flaps fail to move by normal power operation, set the flap lever UP or DOWN as required and use the handpump.

55. **Emergency exits**

For emergency exit the hood(s) should be fully open. If for any reason the hood(s) will not open sufficiently to allow exit, it may be possible to escape through the side panels of the sliding portions, which are jettisoned by pulling down the handle at the centre of the appropriate panel and pushing outwards.

56. Fire-extinguishers

(i) Illumination of the fire warning light (at 68), on the starboard side of either cockpit, indicates a fire at the carburettor intake where the thermocouple-type flame switch is mounted. The extinguishing system, operated by a button also mounted at (68), sprays fluid both into the carburettor intake and from a spray ring on to the back of the engine.

(ii) A hand fire-extinguisher is fitted on the port side of the rear cockpit. When the aircraft is on the ground, it can be reached externally by opening the small door on which it is fitted.

57. Crash landing

(i) Jettison the hood side panels, then open the hood(s) fully.

(ii) Tighten the safety harness.

(iii) Keep the undercarriage retracted.

(iv) Maintain a speed of 85 knots while manœuvring with the flaps up.

(v) Do not lower the flaps until it is certain that the landing ground can be reached under full control. The glide can be lengthened by setting the R.P.M. control lever to the minimum r.p.m. position, when the propeller will move to positive coarse, even if oil pressure is not available.

(vi) Make a straight final approach, under power if possible, at 75-80 knots.

(vii) If time permits before the impact, turn off the fuel, close the throttle and switch off the ignition.

(viii) A crash hand-grip is fitted at the top of the left-hand pillar of each seat.

58. Ditching

In general, the aircraft should be abandoned by parachute rather than ditched. However, if ditching is inevitable:—

(i) Jettison the hood side panels, and then open the hood(s) fully.

(ii) Tighten the safety harness.

(iii) Keep the undercarriage retracted.

(iv) Maintain a speed of 85 knots while manœuvring with the flaps up. If oil pressure is still available, the glide can be lengthened by setting the r.p.m. control lever to positive coarse pitch.

(v) Make a straight final approach, under power if possible, at 70 knots with 20° of flap. The approach should be along the swell, or into wind if the swell is not too steep.

(vi) Touchdown in a tail down attitude at as low a speed as possible.

(vii) A crash hand-grip is fitted at the top of the left-hand pillar of each seat.

59. Signal pistol stowage

(i) The pistol is stowed in the pilot's locker (26), which is located at the bottom of the front instrument panel.

(ii) The cartridges are stowed on the starboard shelf in the front cockpit.

60. First-aid kit

This is stowed on the inside of the baggage compartment door on the port side behind the cockpits.